The Science of DRAGONS

A Field Guide

BRIANNA KAISER

Lerner Publications ◆ Minneapolis

Lerner Publications Company
An imprint of Lerner Publishing Group, Inc.
241 First Avenue North
Minneapolis, MN 55401 USA

For reading levels and more information, look up this title at www.lernerbooks.com.

Main body text set in Aptifer Sans LT Pro.
Typeface provided by Linotype AG.

Editor: Annie Zheng **Designer:** Athena Currier **Photo Editor:** Lucien Brinkley
Lerner team: Martha Kranes

Library of Congress Cataloging-in-Publication Data

Names: Kaiser, Brianna, 1996– author.
Title: The science of dragons : a field guide / Brianna Kaiser.
Description: Minneapolis, MN : Lerner Publications, [2025] | Series: Dragon field guides | Includes bibliographical references and index. | Audience: Ages 8–11. | Audience: Grades 4–6. | Summary: "Some people believe that dragons fly and breathe fire because of magic, but science tells a different story. Young readers discover the science behind dragons, from flight to fire to everyday survival"— Provided by publisher.
Identifiers: LCCN 2024042672 (print) | LCCN 2024042673 (ebook) | ISBN 9798765669303 (library binding) | ISBN 9798765684009 (paperback) | ISBN 9798765676936 (epub)
Subjects: LCSH: Animals, Mythical—Physiology—Juvenile literature. | Dragons—Folklore—Juvenile literature.
Classification: LCC QP81 .K35 2025 (print) | LCC QP81 (ebook) | DDC 398.24/54—dc23/eng/20241119

LC record available at https://lccn.loc.gov/2024042672
LC ebook record available at https://lccn.loc.gov/2024042673

Manufactured in the United States of America
1-1011746-53901-12/16/2024

Table of Contents

A Night Light

It's a quiet night in a valley. The sky is nearly black, making it hard to see much of anything except the moon and stars in the sky. But then a small flame appears in the darkness.

A dragon is breathing fire. The small flame grows until colors of blue, yellow, orange, and red fill the sky. The dragon's fire is so large and bright that it lights up a large part of the valley.

Dragons are not real, but people from all over the world have told stories about dragons for thousands of years. The ideas of how dragons look and act come from these stories.

An illustration of a dragon breathing fire

The stories are different depending on the part of the world they come from. And over time, people's stories of dragons have expanded or changed.

Some people and stories have said dragons can live, breathe fire, and fly because of magic. Other people say dragons can do those things because of science. What do you think?

CHAPTER 1
Survival

Stories have shown that dragons can live all around the world. Usually living alone, some dragons are found in mountains, valleys, or caves. Some live in forests or in bodies of water.

Dragons are apex predators—animals that have few to no enemies and are the top animals of the food chain where they live. Dragons are so big and powerful that they would be hard to kill. But no matter where they live, dragons still need food and water to survive.

Some dragons are said to live in caves and protect treasure.

Food for Energy

Calories are the energy dragons and other animals get from the food they eat. Some people believe that dragons have to eat hundreds of thousands to millions of calories each day

A flock of dragons flying over the mountains

ALONE OR A GROUP?

People believe that most dragons like to live alone. But some books and movies show dragons living in groups.

to provide their bodies with the right amount of energy. If a dragon doesn't eat enough food, it could be low on energy, feel colder than normal, or get sick.

Most dragons in stories are carnivores—animals that eat meat. Dragons eat many types of animals such as deer, horses, cows, and sheep. Dragons that live near water may eat lots of fish. Some dragons do not eat meat. Instead, they eat lots of plants.

Dragons may use their talons, or claws, to tear into prey.

Dragons that live in areas such as deserts may need to search farther for prey.

Since dragons eat so much, they need to live in areas with plenty of food. Some dragons can fly for many hours at a time. But flying uses up more energy, and some dragons cannot fly for as long as others. So it is helpful for a dragon to live near food sources instead of having to fly long distances to find food.

HOT AND COLD

Dragons are large reptiles of myth. Reptiles usually live in warm or tropical places. But dragons can live in hot or cold places.

A group of ice dragons

Search for Water

Dragons likely drink a lot of water, so it is good for them to live near a body of water such as a river, lake, or ocean. The amount of water a dragon needs depends on its size. The larger a dragon is, the more water it needs to drink.

In areas without a lot of water, it is possible that dragons hydrate by drinking the blood of their prey as some real-life animals do.

Dragons can survive for up to two months without eating.

Sometimes a dragon may need to travel far to find water. Most dragons can survive without drinking any water for a few days. Some dragons can go a few weeks or even a month without drinking water.

CHAPTER 2
Breathing Fire

Some dragons breathe acid or poisons. Some dragons breathe frost. But many dragons in books and movies breathe fire.

There are many theories for how dragons can breathe fire. Most of them involve a chemical reaction. A chemical reaction is when one or more chemicals change into other chemicals. These theories are based on the knowledge that fire needs heat, fuel, and oxygen to be able to ignite and keep burning.

Special Parts of the Stomach

Some fire-breathing theories involve a dragon's stomach. In one theory, a dragon stores certain types of chemicals in a special part of its stomach. When the dragon is ready to breathe fire, the chemicals leave that part of the stomach and move into a reaction chamber. Enzymes, or kinds of protein, break down the chemicals in the reaction chamber. The broken-down chemicals heat up to extremely hot temperatures. Then the dragon breathes out the hot fire.

Different-colored fires have different heats. Blue fire is hotter than red fire.

Dragons might also intentionally swallow rocks to help with digestion.

Another theory is that some dragons swallow rocks. When a dragon swallows its food whole, it may also eat rocks by accident. The rocks are stored in the gizzard—a part of a dragon's stomach that grinds down tough foods into smaller pieces. Bones and other tough pieces of food are also stored in the gizzard.

As the food and rocks are broken down in the gizzard, pieces of the rocks break off. The rocks then combine with stomach acids, or fuel. When the combined acids and rocks react with oxygen from the air, flames are created.

MASTERS OF ELEMENTS

In some myths, dragons control elements instead of breathing fire. Some dragons, such as the Chinese long or Japanese ryu, can control wind, water, and rain.

A painting of a Japanese ryu

Special Parts of the Head

Other theories involve a dragon's head and face. In one of these theories, a dragon has a sac in its head that stores acids. When the dragon eats or drinks, it takes in chemicals.

When the chemicals combine with the acids from the sac, they ignite to form fire.

In another theory, dragons have hydrogen glands. Hydrogen is a type of gas, and a gland is a type of body part found in a dragon's head. These special glands provide fuel for fire. Some people believe that dragons have metal or pieces of rocks in their mouths. When these metal and rock

Some scientists believe that dragons share similarities with snakes since some snakes also have a sac in their head that stores venom.

Dragons might breathe fire to defend themselves, communicate, or warn off other dragons.

pieces rub together, they create sparks. Dragons produce fire when hydrogen from the glands reacts with sparks made from rocks the dragons ate.

FACT VS. FICTION

Really large dragons would be too heavy to walk.

FACT and FICTION!

Some people say that large dragons would not be able to support their body weight and that their legs would break. That may be true for dragons that have short legs. But some dragons have long, straight legs like those of huge dinosaurs. These dragons would be able to walk.

An illustration of a brontosaurus

Some people also believe that dragons have a flight bladder. A flight bladder is a part of a dragon's body that is like a second pair of lungs. In one fire-breathing theory, a

Gas in flight bladders helps provide extra lift for dragons when flying.

dragon collects gases in its flight bladder. The dragon can breathe out the gases from its mouth. When the gases meet metals or rocks in the dragon's mouth and oxygen from the air, fire is created.

SHEDDING SKIN

When some dragons grow, their skin doesn't grow with them. If their skin becomes too small, the dragons will shed their skin like a snake.

CHAPTER 3
Taking Flight

When many people think of dragons, they think of dragons flying. Some people think dragons have certain body parts that are made to be lightweight to help the dragon fly. Some light body parts are bones. Dragons have hollow bones filled with air spaces. Other light body parts are air sacs—spaces in a dragon where there is always air. Air sacs store oxygen to power a dragon's muscles for movements such as flight.

Whether they have wings or are wingless, many dragons have the power of flight.

With and Without Wings

When a dragon with wings flies, air moves over the top and bottom of its wings. The shape of the dragon's wings allows air to move faster on the top of the wing than on the bottom, which decreases pressure on the top of the wing. When there is less pressure on top of the wing, it creates an upward force. This lifts the dragon higher into the air.

Dragons need lots of strength to take flight.

When a dragon wants to change direction, it places one wing up and the other wing down. To turn left, the dragon would raise its right wing. To turn right, the dragon would raise its left wing.

Wingless dragons have a skeleton that differs from dragons with wings. The skeletons of wingless dragons allow them to twist and turn easily.

FLIGHT HELP

Some dragons are covered in scales or feathers. Scales could help dragons reduce drag during flight, and feathers could help them steer.

A dragon in a forest

In many stories, dragons without wings have the power to manipulate air so they can fly.

Some wingless dragons fly by riding an air current. An air current is a wind that flows in a certain direction. The air current lifts the dragon into the air.

Some dragons glide instead of fly. These dragons could have unique ribs or other parts of their chest that allow them to glide

A flying dragon descending the mountains

What new dragon science did you learn?

through the air. Dragons that live in water could use their tail to sweep themselves up out of the water and glide in the air.

Your Own Ideas

Now that you've read some theories of how dragons can breathe fire, fly, and survive, what do you think? Is it science or magic? Maybe you think it's a little bit of both, or maybe you have some other ideas. Take some time to reflect on it, and then talk about your ideas with friends.

The ideas you and your friends have about dragons may not be the same. That's okay! People's ideas of dragons have changed throughout history. And coming up with your own ideas for dragon science is half the fun of exploring more about these mythical creatures.

A Look at Long

Long are dragons that come from Chinese myth. Also known as lung or loong, these dragons can live in small or large bodies of water such as rivers and oceans. Even though long don't have wings, they are able to fly. These dragons are often written about or shown in artwork as having horns or antlers, four legs, and bodies covered in scales.

An illustration of a Chinese long

Glossary

drag: a force that opposes the forward motion of flight

element: a force of nature such as air or water

energy: the power or ability to do something

hollow: having an empty space on the inside

ignite: to cause something to begin burning

myth: a story often with imaginative creatures, people, and events that explain history, beliefs, or something else

predator: an animal or creature that hunts other animals or creatures for food

pressure: a force upon a surface

reptile: a cold-blooded animal that lays eggs and often has a body covered in scales or other hard body parts

theory: a view, opinion, or idea presented to explain something

Learn More

Bell, Samantha. *Dragons of Chinese Mythology.* Minneapolis: Kids Core, 2023.

Britannica Kids: Dragon
https://kids.britannica.com/students/article/dragon/274056

Fenmore, Taylor. *Dragons among Us: A Field Guide*. Minneapolis: Lerner Publications, 2026.

Gauthier, Kelly. *The Ultimate Dragon Field Guide: The Fantastical Explorer's Handbook*. Nashville: Applesauce, 2023.

Kiddle: Dragon Facts for Kids
https://kids.kiddle.co/Dragon

Kiddle: Japanese Dragon Facts for Kids
https://kids.kiddle.co/Japanese_dragon

Index

Photo Acknowledgments

Image credits: Coneyl Jay/Getty Images, p. 5; liuzishan/Getty Images, pp. 7, 26; Elle Arden Images/Shutterstock, p. 8; Polina Lopina/Shutterstock, p. 9; Hartmut Witte/Getty Images, p. 10; MasPix/Alamy, pp. 11, 21; Anastelfy/Shutterstock, p. 12; MassyCG/Shutterstock, p. 13; T Studio/Shutterstock, p. 15; Keith Shuttlewood/Alamy, p. 16; Pictures from History/Getty Images, p. 17; dwi septiyana/Getty Images, p. 18; Furiarossa/Shutterstock, p. 19; CSA Images/Getty Images, p. 20; PeartVision/Shutterstock, p. 23; mhd che/Shutterstock, p. 24; touya/Shutterstock, p. 25; digitizesc/Shutterstock, p. 27; vidimages/Getty Images, p. 29. Design elements: NikonLamp/Shutterstock; Lukasz Szwaj/Shutterstock; vi73/Shutterstock; T Studio/Shutterstock; VartB/Shutterstock.

Cover: Arthur Balitskii/Shutterstock.